the
essence
of
style

the essence of
PIERRE DEUX'S
FRENCH COUNTRY

PIERRE MOULIN, PIERRE LE VEC
AND LINDA DANNENBERG

THAMES AND HUDSON

First published in Great Britain in 1995 by Thames and Hudson Ltd. London by arrangement with Clarkson N. Potter, Inc./Publishers, 201 East 50th Street, New York, NY 10022.

British Library Cataloging-in-Publication Data

A catalogue record for this book is available from the British Library.

ISBN 0-500-27853-9

Printed and bound in China

CONTENTS

INTRODUCTION

*The style of the French countryside, with its characteristic warmth, fine craftsmanship, and charm, is beguiling in many provinces of France, but nowhere is it more cohesive and dramatically inspiring than in Provence. This fertile, sun-baked region of southern France, heady with the powerful fragrances of rosemary, lavender, and thyme, boasts an exuberant and lyrical decorative style full of light, color, and harmonious lines—*le style Provençal. *Earthy yet elegant, the style of Provence in furniture, architecture, fabrics, interior design, crafts, and gardens has charmed millions of visitors and influenced thousands of decorators around the world.*

The popular image of French country style, promoted widely over the past two decades by decorators, department stores, and some magazines, is more quaint and rustic than are many of the homes that can actually be found in the French countryside. While there are indeed lovely examples of quaint, rustically furnished cottages, there are also many other moods and styles, from humble farmhouses to historic châteaux, tucked into the hills and dotting rural lanes.

The style of the French countryside has evolved over hundreds of years, passing through myriad design influences and arriving at a look that is appealingly genuine and perfectly adapted to its time and place. Within the cottages, châteaux, and farmhouses of Provence, there is little effort to make everything "match," or even to maintain a continuity of periods. The French mix what they like with what they need with what the family has handed down. The look is eclectic and yet cohesive, a welcoming mix of color, texture, substance, and light.

Although open to broad interpretation (which is why it can be adapted so admirably), French country style does have some basic markings. French country is not delicate crystal and porcelain, but rather the chunky, mouth-blown glass of Biot and the hand-molded faïence of Moustiers. It is not pale embossed silks and satins, but vibrantly patterned cottons. It is not fragile gilded and upholstered chairs, but *rather the rush-seated banquettes from Uzès, embellished with a naïve floral bouquet and designed for family living. And it is not the sleek, symmetrical slate roofs of a Paris town house, but rather the undulating, mottled tiles on a patchwork of roofs tipped at odd angles in Loumarin.*

Never stylized, never contrived, and never pretentious, true French country style is exceedingly easy to live with. And it travels beautifully, adapting to a variety of environments far from its roots in the Gallic provinces. Using provincial colors, fabrics, furniture, and decorative objects, as well as the imagination that characterizes the style at its source, you can create the French country look virtually anywhere. The mistral may not howl down your chimney, and the sun may not be a shimmering aura outside your windows, but the exuberant spirit of the French countryside will be within, and the charm will be there too.

PRECEDING PAGES: *Pots of geraniums brighten an old stone well in the courtyard of the Château de Fontarèches near Uzès.*

Looking Outside

THE *finest Provençal homes, be they humble or grand, are true to their territory. In a shady village in the Bouches-du-Rhône, in the rolling countryside of the Vaucluse, or on the hot, dry plains of the Camargue, the houses are at one with the land—in proportion to their surroundings, constructed from local materials, and in character with their neighbors. The abundant local sandstone and limestone enhance and strengthen many façades, particularly around a house's apertures. Doors and windows, sometimes entire façades, are also embellished by dazzling color, used liberally and with great zest.*

The warm, rich, intense colors of Provence are the colors of the earth, the flowers, the sky, and the sea. The characteristic ochres, russets, silver-greens, cerulean blues, deep roses, alizarin reds, sunflower yellows, and lavenders of the land and the waters of the Mediterranean are picked up and adapted in fabrics, furniture, tiles, and interior and exterior décor. The gentle flow of color from the outside in and from the inside out—between the colors of nature and the colors of man—is another example of the harmony that typifies this area.

Augmenting the colors splashed by nature across the Provençal terrain are the gardens, little or lavish, that brighten almost every property in the region. The gardens of the Midi might be described most succinctly as patches and pots of brilliance. Bursts of startling, vivid color punctuate windowsills, doorways, backyard paths, poolside embankments, balconies, and terraces. From Menton to Moustiers to Les Saintes-Maries-de-la-Mer, roses, eglantines, jasmine, petunias, acacias, laurel, marguerites, lavender, and, of course, hearty geraniums bloom in a fragrant carnival of color. Almost everywhere you turn in Provence, your eye will almost certainly come to rest on a flower.

PRECEDING PAGES: *In the rolling hills of the Basses-Alpes, near the famous pottery town of Moustiers, a hazy late-afternoon sun burnishes fields of lavender and wheat.*

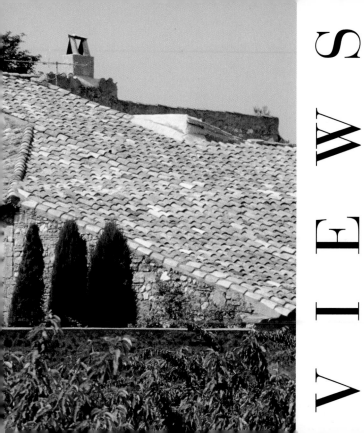

VIEWS

ABOVE: *A cluster of terra-cotta canal-tile roofs dominates the view of a small hill town north of Aix-en-Provence.* **PRECEDING PAGES:** *Slanting in all directions, the mottled tile roofs of a Renaissance* mas, *or farmhouse, in the little town of Mouriès, testify to the structure's organic growth over the centuries.*

BELOW: *In a touch of agricultural whimsy, a scarecrow dressed as a gendarme sternly guards an apricot orchard in Les Baux-de-Provence.*

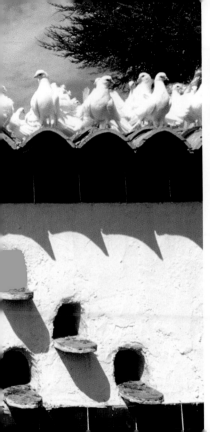

Behind the Mas de Cacherel,
a sprawling ranch in the
Camargue—France's cowboy
country—a stylish colom-
bier, or dovecote, with a
green enamel tile border and
a canal-tile roof, is home to
a large flock of pure white
fantail doves.

19

FAR LEFT: *A steep little street leads to the old town behind the modern city of Nice.*

CLOCKWISE FROM TOP LEFT: *Canal tiles slant down to the pool of a home near Gordes; a serene pavillon in Les Baux-de-Provence dates from the mid-1500s; a pale blue façade stands in Saint-Rémy.*

OPPOSITE PAGE, TOP RIGHT: *Sober in natural stone is an antiquated dovecote near Avignon.* **OPPOSITE PAGE AND ABOVE:** *In Le Vieux Nice, the Old Town of Nice, residents use a free hand and a blithe spirit in adorning their houses with color—here, washes of rose and gold.*

LEFT: *Dried wheat, potted ferns, and ivy coexist on a stone wall within a restored 18th-century home in Moustiers.* **ABOVE:** *A well-worn path connects a family compound in the town of Le Paradou.*

LEFT: *An* allée *of majestic plane trees leads to the Château de Roussan, an 18th-century mansion near Saint-Rémy that is now a hotel.* **ABOVE:** *The entrance to the* colombier *on the grounds of the Château de Barbentane bears a carved label.*

27

CLOCKWISE FROM TOP LEFT: *Sulfur-blue shutters in Mouriès close out the summer sun; elaborate carvings embellish an apartment in Le Vieux Nice; a hand-painted shield marks an antiques shop in Fontvieille.* **FAR RIGHT:** *Pink geraniums line the sill atop a horsemeat butcher's shop in old Saint-Rémy.*

EXTERIORS

Below: *Beneath a diamond-shaped aperture, a wrought-iron lantern illuminates the entrance of a home near Saint-Rémy.*
Preceding pages: *Geraniums bloom outside a ranch-hand's simple cottage in the Camargue.*

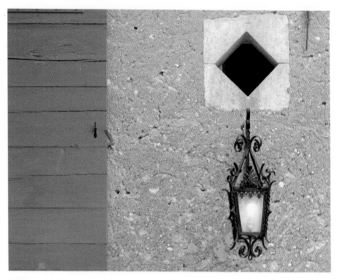

ABOVE: *Matching wood-plank shutters and door, painted olive, accent a stone farmhouse in Saint-Rémy; the wood-bead curtain, called a* rideau de buis, *ubiquitous in Provence, lets in air but keeps out flies.*

CLOCKWISE FROM TOP LEFT: *A distinctive variety of apertures keeps out heat and light in a 19th-century home in Le Paradou, in an elegant home in Eygalières, and in a simple village house in Les Baux-de-Provence.* **FAR RIGHT:** *A deeply recessed fan window admits light to a 19th-century building in Nice.*

ABOVE: *A handmade trellis rests against the stone wall of a 15th-century* mas *near Les Baux-de-Provence.*
RIGHT: *On the back façade of the Château de Fontarèches, a little stone fountain trickles water next to the architectural remnant of an obsolete archway.*

Above: *Lace-curtained French doors lead into a modest stone carriage house in Maillane.* **Right:** *The tall double doors of this elegant village home near Gordes open directly onto a view of the back garden and pool.*

LEFT: *The numerous doors of an 18th-century house near Saint-Rémy bear witness to its original incarnation as a large stable.* **ABOVE:** *Steps through a garden archway near Eygalières lead to a back door topped by a classic* oeil-de-boeuf *window.*

ABOVE: *The arched French doors of a wine-producer's home in Eygalières are protected by sturdy latching shutters.* **RIGHT:** *The mullioned windows of a Renaissance mas in Mouriès remain bare of shutters, which the owners felt would detract from the home's classic 16th-century character, with its beautiful stonework.*

LEFT: *The soft pink color of a home in Le Paradou comes from the natural tones of a sand-based daub that was used instead of paint.* **ABOVE:** *The entrance to the sprawling Mas de Cacherel in the Camargue is a small vertical-plank door flanked by two enormous rosemary bushes.*

45

GARDENS

48

LEFT: *Intricately carved in stone, an 18th-century basket heaped with fruit decorates a garden wall.* **ABOVE:** *A sculpted* tête de grotesque, *or gargoyle head, spouts water into a lily-filled trough in a garden in Uzès.* **PRECEDING PAGES:** *Robust 18th-century peasant figures carved out of limestone rest next to an old pool on the grounds of the Château de Roussan near Saint-Rémy.*

RIGHT AND PRECEDING PAGES:
Carved out of the region's abundant limestone, sandstone, and occasionally marble, a vast range of stone sculptures grace gardens and pools throughout Provence. Romantic and allegorical figures were favorite subjects, as were urns, fruit baskets, and small gargoyles; even old grinding wheels take on sculptural qualities. These decorative garden projects were treats for local stonemasons, most of whose work was architectural; they loved to flaunt their masterly techniques, learned from itinerant Italian sculptors in the 17th and 18th centuries.

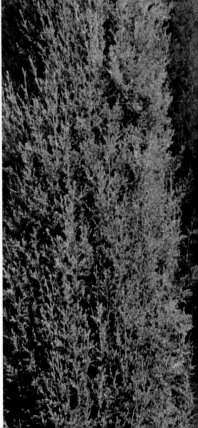

ABOVE AND RIGHT: *A wrought-iron trellis leads into the vast gardens of a Renaissance* mas *in Mouriès. A pair of cypresses marks the begin-ning of the* allée *through the vegetable garden, where the vegetables are bordered by flowers.*

*Clustered pots of flowers
form the garden of a small
home in Le Paradou, ABOVE,
and brighten the stone back
stairway of the Château de
Fontarèches in Uzès, RIGHT.*

LEFT: *The orangerie of the Château de Barbentane, near Avignon, opens onto a small contemporary pool.* **BELOW:** *An abandoned bakehouse overgrown with ivy and grapevines overlooks the garden pool of the Château de Roussan.*

LEFT: *The* orangerie *of the Château de Barbentane houses a variety of potted plants in various stages of development.* **ABOVE:** *Red and white laurels, ubiquitous in Lower Provence, add vibrant color to a garden path near Fontvieille.*

ABOVE, LEFT AND RIGHT: *A large pottery urn and an old painted barrel holding geraniums in a multitude of hues accent the garden of a modest home in the small, shady town of Maussane, close to Les Baux-de-Provence.*

Above left: *At a mas in Mouriès, an urn of geraniums set on a stone pedestal is camouflaged by a mound of ivy trained around it.* **Above right:** *Volcanic boulders set the stage for an array of geraniums in a garden near Fontvieille.*

The back stairway of the somber limestone Château de Fontarèches in Uzès is brightened by a lushly blooming hydrangea bush, its vibrant pinks in dramatic contrast to the greige-toned stone and brown door.

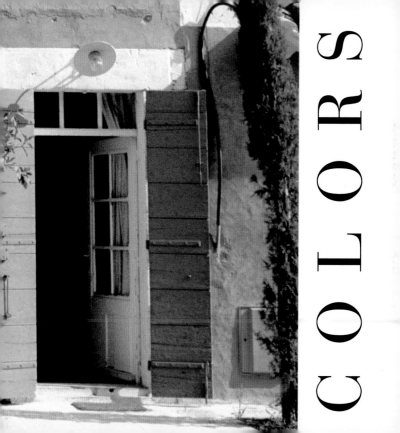

COLORS

LEFT: *A renovated* mas *in Saint-Rémy is newly painted a deep rosy pink, with French blue doors surrounded by a stark white border.* **ABOVE:** *An old agricultural thermometer hangs in contrast to the russet siding of a barn in Maillane.* **PRECEDING PAGES:** *The vivid rose and turquoise colors of Régine Deméry's 240-year-old house in Le Paradou reflect the bright, welcoming personality of its owner.*

ABOVE: *One of Van Gogh's favorite subjects, the sunflowers of Provence, which turn their faces to follow the sun, here face west in the late afternoon.* **RIGHT:** *A giant chrysanthemum in a garden near Saint-Rémy rivals nearby sunflowers with its own blaze of golden color.*

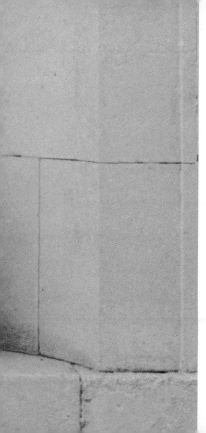

LEFT: *Within a tranquil niche in a Saint-Rémy garden, geraniums sprout from a traditional Provençal green pottery urn produced in Fontvieille.* **ABOVE:** *A cherry orchard near L'Isle-sur-la-Sorgue makes a serene setting for a summer picnic.*

LEFT: *A 19th-century yellow faïence plate produced near L'Isle-sur-la-Sorgue rests on a cherry-patterned boutis, or quilt, from the mid-1800s.*
ABOVE: *Zinnias, marigolds, and marguerites are among the hearty blooms that flourish in a garden near Les Baux-de-Provence.*

The colors of a small 18th-century house in Le Paradou derive from ochre (iron ore) and red bauxite, found in the nearby hills.

A wash of mustard yellow enlivens the walls of a humble store-house next to a quaint cottage in Maussane. Clustered pots of flowers somewhat camouflage the peeling façade.

A dazzling multicolored patchwork created from ceramic tiles from François Vernin in Apt forms a unique backsplash for a small sink in Jean-Pierre Deméry's home in Le Paradou.

LEFT: *Trellised grapevines are dappled—and protected from pests—by pale blue copper sulfate spray.* **ABOVE:** *Outside a café in the Vieux Port, or Old Harbor, of Marseilles, a stack of chairs in a shade of blue that rivals the nearby Mediterranean awaits the start of a busy day.*

Striking shades of blue catch the eye on the shutters of a farmhouse near Saint-Rémy and on the unique façade of an egg and poultry shop in Nice, covered in a mosaic dating from the 1930s.

LOOKING INSIDE

THE graceful lines and generous spirit of Provence characterize the interiors of the region's traditional homes. There was no guiding aesthetic theory in 18th- and 19th-century Provence, and yet all the components of a classic and eclectic Provençal room have the harmony and coherence of a structured style. The artisans, architects, and artists who created what grew into le style Provençal were simply responding to the needs, the desires, and the spirit of a people in a very particular time and place.

One of the first things that strikes you upon entering a traditional Provençal home is the beamed or slatted ceiling. Massive hand-hewn beams and slats called rondins, which are interspersed with plaster, give a sturdy rustic charm to cottages and farmhouses. Also dominant in a spare, often whitewashed room is the generously proportioned fireplace made of plaster, or, in grander domains, of stone or marble.

Keeping a house temperate—cool in the blazing, dry summer and warm during a winter of chill winds—has always been a concern in Provencçal house design. The *ubiquitous terra-cotta floor tiles of the region are thus an attractive, economical, and very practical choice for flooring.*

Vibrantly beautiful, lavishly patterned Provençal cottons fill the rooms with distinctive color, style, and soul. Complementing the fabrics, and repeating many printed motifs of flowers and vines in masterfully carved, burnished woods, is the graceful and handsomely wrought furniture of Provence. The luminous faïence of Moustiers, Apt, and many other small towns, has lines as fluid and classic as the furniture on which the hand-molded pieces are displayed. As with so many other aspects of Provençal décor, the faïence reflects an unquenchable joie de vivre.

PRECEDING PAGES: *Rustic and sophisticated elements coexist in a restored 16th-century house in Les Bories, with terra-cotta floors, a massive stonework fireplace, Oriental rugs, and 19th-century upholstered armchairs.*

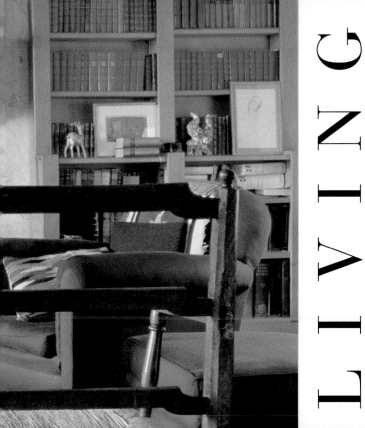

LIVING

LEFT: *Rose-toned Provençal cottons enhance the living room of a small cottage.* **ABOVE:** *A stand originally designed to hold a pitcher of water works here as a sturdy end table.* **PRECEDING PAGES:** *An 18th-century banquette sits across from the wide stone fireplace in the living room of a house in Ménèrbes.*

LEFT: *In whimsical juxta-position, a Mediterranean Directoire wrought-iron chair flanks a massive 18th-century gilt-framed mirror reflecting an Art Deco sculpture in the facing bathroom.*
PRECEDING PAGES: *A diverse array of provincial 18th- and 19th-century chairs—upholstered, rush-seated, and woven rattan—populates the salons, studies, and bedrooms of country dwellings, both humble and grand.*

LEFT: *A 19th-century provincial armoire serves as a copiously filled cabinet.* **ABOVE:** *Rustic turn-of-the-century rush-seated chairs painted white, a 19th-century French baker's rack, and bistro mirrors all contribute to the unusual décor of a lavish pool house.*

Above: *A marble-topped 18th-century Provençal table backs a large contemporary sofa covered in quilted muslin in a restored home near Gordes.* **Right:** *In a living room in Le Paradou, an eclectic group of elegant chairs surrounds a graceful 18th-century game table.*

ABOVE: *In the diminutive living room of a cottage, a Louis XVI armchair sits between the fireplace framed in blue-and-white Italian tiles and a farm table of mixed woods.* **RIGHT:** *Oversized cushions covered in Souleiado cottons are part of the eclectic veranda décor of a village home in LeParadou.*

CLOCKWISE FROM TOP LEFT: *A stone-walled salon in Mouriès; the comfortable living room of a ranch in the Camargue; a 19th-century buffet as an elegant bar.* **FAR RIGHT:** *A side chair is topped by a cushion and a doll, both clad in Provençal cottons.*

LEFT: *In one of the stylish bathrooms in the Château de Fontarèches, a rush-seated late 18th-century "nursing chair" provides a low seat next to a sleek marble fireplace.* **ABOVE:** *An early 18th-century leather box decorated with brass angels and birds.*

103

ABOVE: *A sturdy late 19th-century provincial dessert table adds character to a spare contemporary country house.* **RIGHT:** *An antique American quilt covers a carved Empire bed in a wood-paneled bedroom.*

Above: *Handworked lace curtains, woven in northern Provence about 1880, cover a small bedroom window.*
Right: *Lace curtains drape the bedroom window of a small house in Tarascon, while hand-blocked Provençal cotton curtains remain open at the side.*

LEFT: *A subdued mixture of Provençal fabrics and patterns defines a country living room.* **ABOVE:** *A rustic 18th-century seat for three, painted with flowers but missing a rung, has pride of place in the foyer of a château near Avignon.*

LEFT: *Harmonizing with a tub of dried lavender, a collection of antique blue quilts hangs by a rustic blue peasant armoire from Haute Provence.* **ABOVE:** *This intricately quilted 19th-century coverlet with a rich floral border, was created for a bride's trousseau.*

ABOVE: *In the library of a home near Gordes, a large sulfur ball, which once helped a 19th-century shopkeeper keep an eye on customers, reflects more than 180 degrees of the room.* **RIGHT:** *Small collections and souvenirs fill the billiard room of an estate in Maillane.*

LEFT: *White walls and clear glass doors brighten a village house near Gordes.* **PRECEDING PAGES:** *Vignettes of style and taste demonstrate the comfortable integration of antique furniture—some of it dating back to the 18th century—into Provençal homes; the colorful presence of flowers and potted plants adds to the easy-going charms of these interiors.*

ABOVE: *A Provençal boutis, or quilt, covers a table by the window of a bedroom in an 18th-century house in Maillane.* **RIGHT:** *At the back of the black-and-white tiled foyer in the Maillane house, a graceful stairway with an 18th-century banister winds up to the second floor.*

LEFT: *An interior stone stair-case connects the first and second floors of a 16th-century town house in Ménèrbes.* **ABOVE:** *A lacy, intricately worked wrought-iron railing adds a romantic Mediterranean allure to the second floor of an 18th-century house near Saint-Rémy.*

On a small side table in the living room of an estate near Saint-Rémy, the owner proudly displays his collection of carved bears.

LEFT: *In a sunny foyer, a small 18th-century armchair keeps company with a 19th-century nightstand, serving here as a telephone table.* **ABOVE:** *A mélange of vibrant pink prints enlivens a living room in Le Paradou. A clear plastic trunk filled with antique quilts does duty as an end table.*

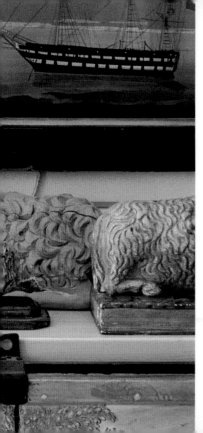

In a blue and white–themed cottage, the living room mantel displays a collection of carved French and Italian lambs, as well as blue-glazed faïence and porcelain.

ABOVE: *A rustic provincial table converted from a small bench serves as a coffee table in front of a contemporary sofa in white linen.*
RIGHT: *Adjacent to a garden pool, an alcove veranda holds a slatted all-weather sofa with quilted cushions.*

DINING

LEFT: *In a light-bathed dining room in Les Bories, the luncheon table is set with a first course of melon and Bayonne ham.* **ABOVE:** *An unusual faïence candelabrum graces a luncheon table; the tiny melons are the celebrated produce of Cavaillon.* **PRECEDING PAGES:** *A farm table awaits guests for Sunday supper.*

133

LEFT: *For an alfresco dinner, the table is laid with a vivid tablecloth by Pierre Frey and balloon-patterned soup dishes from Moustiers.* **ABOVE:** *Beneath the beamed dining room ceiling of an old estate, a huge 17th-century convent table is surrounded by late 19th-century Provençal side chairs.*

ABOVE: *In preparation for an outdoor buffet, two antique park chairs flank a marble-topped Victorian table.* **RIGHT:** *By a kitchen window in the Camargue, a 19th-century kneading table displays local faïence and apothecary bottles.*

136

LEFT: *A small table in Le Paradou is laid with garnet-toned faïence plates and Provençal cotton napkins.*
BELOW: *In a former pantry, a Directoire monastery table extends from an inset 19th-century glass cupboard.*

The marble floors of the lavish, luminous dining room of the Château de Barbentane near Avignon, created in a sophisticated trompe l'oeil pattern, reflect the influence of Italian artisans who worked in Provence in the early 18th century. Also crafted in marble is the sensuous Louis XV mantel.

LEFT: *In a sunny breakfast room, four provincial Louis XVI side chairs surround a 19th-century table from Champagne.* **ABOVE:** *At a Bastille Day dinner, the table is set with a Provençal print cloth and faïence plates with French Revolutionary symbols.*

141

In a handsome Franco-American alliance, American Windsor chairs surround a massive 19th-century French farm table in a flower-sprigged dining room. Partially glimpsed on the left is an elaborately carved 18th-century oak armoire from Normandy.

LEFT: *In a dining room in Maillane, a collection of turn-of-the-century plates covers one wall. A set of turn-of-the-century side chairs in walnut encircle the dining room table.* **ABOVE:** *An 18th-century* buffet provençal *serves as the base of a small bar set*

145

Under a tree laden with apricots, a table covered with a contemporary Souleiado cloth is set for traditional Provençal aperitifs in the garden: tiny ceramic bowls of green olives, matching bowls of ice cubes, a pitcher of water, and a bottle of Pernod—the classic pastis cocktail so refreshing on a hot, dry day.

In a back garden near Gordes, a variation on the typical Provençal aperitifs includes a wine punch, glasses filled with ice, lemon and mint sprigs, and bowls of wafer cookies and pre-served cherries, arranged on a wrought-iron table sur-rounded by matching chairs

In the Camargue, a Provençal tomato juice cocktail is created by macerating sliced lemons and a handful of fresh mint in a pitcher of tomato juice for about three hours; alone or spiked with gin or vodka, it's an extremely pleasing hot-weather aperitif.

A sumptuous French country picnic covers a long farm table for a casual indoor dinner party: crusty loaves of peasant bread, crisp baguettes, platters of Bayonne ham, pâté, saucisson sec, spicy terrines and other charcuterie, platters of assorted cheeses—chèvre, Camembert, Brie, Cantal, Pyrénées—bowls of tomatoes and fresh basil dressed with Dijon vinaigrette, bowls of niçoise olives, and, of course, plentiful carafes of hearty red Côtes du Rhône wines.

COOKING

ABOVE: *A new batch of pickled cherries rests on one of the hemp filters for olive oil presses widely used in Provence as placemats.* **RIGHT:** *Green enamel tile and brickwork accent a rustic kitchen in Le Paradou.* **PRECEDING PAGES:** *Within an 18th-century kitchen fireplace in Maillane stands a professional stainless steel stove.*

LEFT: *The drawers along the wall of a farmhouse kitchen near Saint-Rémy were once part of a local grocery shop.* **ABOVE:** *In a small village kitchen, an 18th-century storage cabinet holds two old vinegar kegs.*

ABOVE: *Provençal faïence plates drain next to a 19th-century polished stone sink in the corner of a wine-producer's kitchen in Bandol.* **RIGHT:** *Antique blue-and-white Provençal tiles have been set into a long rustic farm table in the dining room of the Mas de Cacherel in the Camargue.*

ABOVE: *A provincial spoon-holder hangs like a mobile in the center of a small kitchen.*
RIGHT: *In a contemporary kitchen composed largely of antique French elements, a 19th-century copper pail holds cooking implements next to a glazed terrine and an earthenware casserole.*

162

Above: *The center of a home near Saint-Rémy is the fragrant kitchen, hung with bunches of dried herbs and flowers.* **Right:** *Faïence tiles with a French Revolution motif form a backsplash to a small gas stove.*

LEFT: *Large tiles glazed in lush deep green compose the kitchen counter of the Château de Fontarèches in Uzès.* **BELOW:** *Old santons—Provençal ceramic figurines—form a pretty still life on a kitchen windowsill in Le Paradou.*

LEFT: *The morning sun shines on large bottles of home-made red wine vinegar stored on a kitchen shelf next to a 19th-century vinegar keg.* **ABOVE:** *A collection of 19th-century partially glazed ceramic pots from the Dordogne, displayed along the top of the built-in cabinets, adds a rustic touch to a contemporary kitchen.*

The heart of the rural Provençal home is the fireplace, which traditionally served as the main source of heat as well as the cooking center. This hearth in Moustiers is equipped with hooks and andirons.

ABOVE: *In the Domaine de Tempier in Bandol, a hand-blocked border print of Provençal fabric above the fireplace serves to keep smoke from fanning out into the kitchen.* **RIGHT:** *Antique rush-seated chairs dress up a simple farm table in the kitchen of the Château de Fontarèches.*

LEFT: *In the kitchen of the Mas de Cacherel, where antique blue-and-white tiles predominate, an open storage area under the sink is simply covered by red-checked cotton curtains.* **ABOVE:** *Adding visual interest as well as a sturdy work surface to a mixed-woods country kitchen is an old and well-used French butcher's table.*

173

SLEEPING

Above: *In the guest bedroom of a home near Gordes, a dressmaker's muslin is used for bedspread and pillow covers.* **Right:** *In a feminine bedroom, linens from Porthault cover the bed.* **Preceding pages:** *This variation of the canopy bed was fashionable in the mid-19th century.*

FAR LEFT: *Red-and-white print fabrics complement a hand-blocked coverlet from India at the foot of a bed.* **CLOCKWISE FROM TOP LEFT:** *Antique French lace curtains diffuse light; a half-canopy in blue and white adds a romantic touch; paisley print by Souleiado curtains a small bedroom.*

LEFT: *In a bedroom near L'Isle-sur-la-Sorgue, the painted bed was carved in Aix-en-Provence around 1890.* **ABOVE:** *In the bedroom of a home near Gordes, a stylized canopy bed was fashioned from plumbing pipes painted in panther spots.*

*An airy master bedroom in tones of white and beige is bright-
ened by a canopy bed hung with Provençal cottons from
Souleiado.*

In a rural country bedroom, blue-and-white Provençal cotton covers the old walls, and assorted Provençal throw pillows add a dash of color to the quilted white bedspread. The desk chair is a Restoration armchair from Provence.

In a guest bedroom of the *Mas de Cacherel, the simply carved bed is a 19th-century* litoche, *with bedcoverings made from a 1950s copy of an 18th-century toile de Jouy.*

LEFT: *In a 16th-century house in Ménèrbes, the walls are decorated with murals painted by a local 19th-century itinerant artist.* **ABOVE:** *An Empire-style bed serves as a sofa in a bedroom in the Mas de Cacherel. A 19th-century corner cabinet holds a large spray of roses.*

187

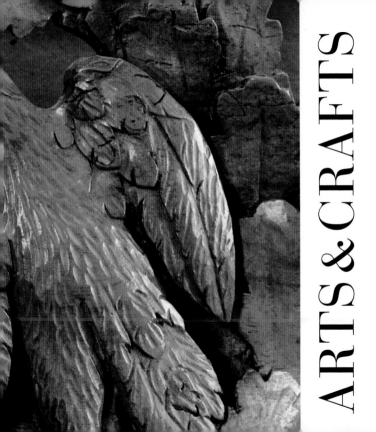

ARTS&CRAFTS

CLOCKWISE FROM TOP LEFT: *Graceful simplicity characterizes the work of 18th- and 19th-century Provençal cabinetmakers.* **FAR RIGHT:** *Four Provençal flour boxes display a variety of characteristic motifs.* **PRECEDING PAGES:** *A unique carving of a fox and a stork was inspired by a fable by La Fontaine.*

ABOVE: *The carved detailing of an 18th-century armoire crafted in Arles displays a musical theme, featuring sheet music, a lyre, and a hunting horn.* **RIGHT:** *A handsome, beautifully patinaed 18th-century walnut commode has three concave drawers with elaborate copper pulls fashioned into Provençal bouquets.*

Left: *In the antique color-spattered laboratory of the Souleiado company in Tarascon, windows are permanently splashed with a kaleidoscope of experimental dyes.* **Above:** *Régine Deméry of Souleiado develops a new design in one of the firm's studios.*

LEFT: *Demonstrations of how hand-blocked fabrics were printed take place at Souleiado's Tarascon headquarters. The cut-copper block in the foreground is used first to print a fabric's black outline; the colors are then printed sequentially:* **ABOVE:** *Measuring utensils hang over the stone sink in the Souleiado color kitchen.*

ABOVE: *New Provençal cottons are designed at Souleiado using components from old blocks. All prototypes are done by hand on cellophane.* **RIGHT:** *The Souleiado Museum's textile archives include a phenomenal collection of 40,000 hand-carved blocks.*

LEFT: *The Souleiado archives also include books of rare swatches of 18th- and 19th-century* indiennes, *Provençal fabrics inspired by hand-printed cottons from India.*
BELOW: *Textile workers pose in Souleiado's Tarascon work-room, circa 1905.*

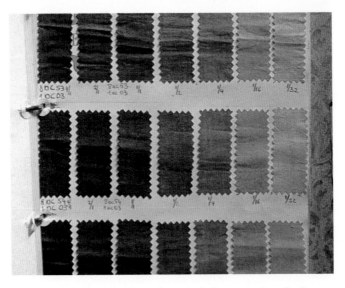

ABOVE: *Part of Souleiado's archives includes a catalog of color swatches in every imaginable hue; here, a page of blues.* **RIGHT:** *In L'Isle-sur-la-Sorgue, a collection of Provençal boutis, or quilts, made between 1820 and 1870, airs in the morning sun.*

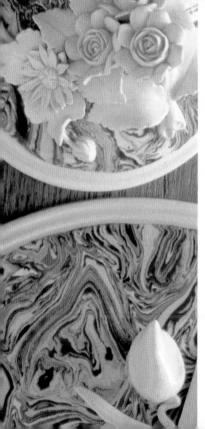

LEFT: *Three marbleized clay pots, made in Apt in the early 1900s using 18th-century techniques, testify to the craftsmanship of Bernard Faucon, founder of the Atelier Bernard, today run by his grandson, Jean Faucon.* **ABOVE:** *At the Atelier de Ségriès in Apt, hand-thrown pitchers of red clay are dipped into a first coat of white glaze.*

203

CLOCKWISE FROM TOP LEFT: *At the Atelier de Ségriès in Moustiers, a potter forms a pitcher from the red clay of Roussillon; recently fired faïence cools in the kiln; a rare figure from the late 1700s has a richly detailed costume of brocades.* **FAR RIGHT:** *Papier-mâché carnival masks date from the early 1800s.*

LEFT: *Marbleized clay faïence, made at Jean Faucon's studio in Apt, is displayed atop and above an 18th-century Provençal buffet.* **ABOVE:** *Also characteristic of Apt faïence are these scalloped yellow-glazed plates, hand-molded by Jean Faucon.*

Also available in the *Essence of Style* series